TAKING CHARGE OF MY LIFE

CHOICES, CHANGES AND ME

By Ed Harmon and Marge Jarmin

Cartoons by Larry Feign

The Barksdale Foundation
P.O. Box 187
Idyllwild, California 92549

Cover and production by Deborah Carlson

Printed in the United States of America
First Printing, September 1988
Second Printing, April 1992

Library of Congress Cataloging-in-Publication Data

Harmon, Ed, 1930-
  Taking charge of my life.

  1. Youth—Conduct of life. I. Jarmin,
Marge, 1941- .II. Feign, Larry.
III. Title.
BJ1661.H22 1988   158'.1   88-988
ISBN 0-918588-10-3

The Barksdale Foundation
P.O. Box 187, Idyllwild, CA 92549
(909) 659-4676
Visit us on the Internet at
http://www.barksdale.org

This book is lovingly dedicated to the memory of
Lilburn S. "Barks" Barksdale
whose ideas on human behavior inspired us to write it.

ABOUT THE AUTHORS

Ed Harmon, Ph.D.—Dr. Harmon's background combines academic preparation in science and engineering at Case Western Reserve University with extensive experience in industrial management and human resources development, including eight years conducting Barksdale Self-Esteem Workshops for adults. He teaches college and university courses in human development, learning theory and teacher survival skills. He is co-developer of the Conner and Harmon systems model of human experience.

Marge Jarmin, M.A.—Ms. Jarmin holds a master's degree in psychology from the University of Redlands, as well as current California elementary and secondary teaching credentials. Over 20 years experience as an educator has given her a wealth of knowledge and experience in dealing with young people and their needs. She is an educational consultant for public and private elementary and secondary schools, providing staff development training in self-esteem. Marge also conducts trainings for peer counseling groups as well as offering classes and private consultations for teens and preteens in decision making and self-esteem.

Together these two professionals are shedding new light on how young people can create happy, caring, and productive lives.

ACKNOWLEDGMENTS

The authors are grateful to Jan Burnett for editing the manuscript. Her patience, caring, and diligence were an invaluable contribution.

The encouragement and vision of Charlene Brown provided the inspiration and energy to get started on the project. For these we are deeply appreciative.

TABLE OF CONTENTS

Preface

PREFACE

A Message for Youth

We have written this book for *you,* to assist you in having the life you want. We know you are under a lot of pressure from your friends to "fit in," from your teachers to achieve your potential, and from your parents to live up to the values they have taught you. It's easy to feel you're a victim, living your life for everyone else.

We want you to know that this is your life and that you are in charge of it. We won't be trying to "fix" you; *you* don't need fixing. We will be giving you ideas that you can use to help you understand what you can and cannot control in your life so you'll be happier and more likely to get what you want.

The best way to use this book is first to read it from beginning to end and not skip around since the ideas in each chapter build on the ones that come before it. Doing the exercises as you come to them will help you use the ideas for your own benefit, so you will not just know about being happy, you'll have a way to become happier.

Later you may want to refer to certain parts of the book for help in resolving particular problems. The last chapter is a short review of the whole book so you may want to read it from time to time for a quick refresher.

We want you to know that we sincerely care about you. We believe that you can both enjoy your life and also be successful at what you do. The first step is knowing that you have a *choice!*

A Message for Concerned, Caring Adults

As school drop-outs, unwanted pregnancies, substance abuse, and teen suicide escalate to alarming levels, the need to enable young people to make choices that lead to healthy, productive lives has become increasingly urgent. Past focus has been on symptoms rather than causes, with few positive changes coming out of that approach. In this book we offer tools for eliminating the *causes* of destructive behavior, and for helping young people deal effectively with the many pressures they face today.

A major cause of destructive behavior is low self-esteem. When kids reject themselves they are more likely to give in to peer pressure in order to feel wanted and to belong. They are more likely to abuse alcohol, drugs or food in an attempt to relieve the feelings of guilt and unworthiness that self-rejection produces. Low self-esteem also creates strong needs to control, to be right and to make others wrong in order to compensate for feelings of inadequacy. Ultimate feelings of self-rejection tragically result in teen suicide.

When young people think they have no choices, they feel helpless and victimized, unable to experience their worth and importance. The need to compensate for these feelings often occurs and may result in strong antisocial behaviors. These behaviors will diminish, if not disappear, when kids realize that they are not victims, that they do have options, and that they are in charge of their actions, feelings, and future. As caring adults, we can assist young people by helping them form the habit of exploring choices and consequences.

Internalizing and applying the ideas in this book will enable young people to make positive life style changes. They will become more eager to participate in life rather than escape from it. They will be more willing to set long-range goals and work to achieve them. Feeling they are worthwhile, lovable human beings will result in greater cooperation with their family, friends, teachers, and society.

It will accelerate young people's understanding when you, as an adult, can model the concepts presented in this book. Sharing and working through the ideas together can be enjoyable and tremendously helpful in creating open, loving relationships with the young people in your life.

CHAPTER ONE

ACCEPTING YOUR OWN AUTHORITY

We have a suggestion for you on how to approach the ideas in this book. Here it is.

Don't believe any of it!

If you believe something is true, and it isn't true,

then you are stuck with the consequences of your false belief.

We suggest that instead of "believing" what you read in this book,

you check it out for yourself, using your own experience and your own ability to think.

The purpose of this book is not to give you advice,

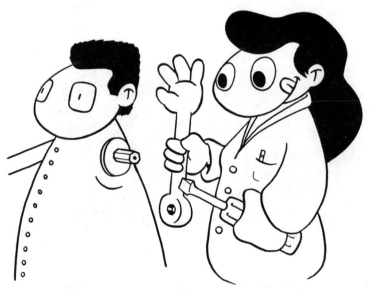

or to fix you.

We suspect you've had more than enough of that in your life already.

We just want to share with you what we've found out about how people's lives *really* work.

You'll be shown what might be called a map that you can use, if you like, to help you make choices in your life. We'll share ideas about how we human beings operate. We suggest that you check out these ideas to see if they make sense to you, to find out if you

agree,

disagree,

or haven't decided yet.

By the time you complete this book you will have some practical tools that you can start using in your life; immediately if you want,

or you can choose not to use them. It's up to you.

1. Have you ever done something you didn't want to do, but had to do?

2. Is there anyone who has the power to make you angry or upset?

3. Have you ever done something you shouldn't have done?

How would you answer these three questions?

Question No. 1

HAVE YOU EVER DONE SOMETHING YOU DIDN'T **WANT** TO DO, BUT **HAD** TO DO?

Have you ever done something you didn't *want* to do, but *had* to do? If you answered "yes" to this question, you have a lot of company.

We've asked many thousands of people this question. More than 98 out of 100 answer "YES!" Some of the most common things that teens say are:

"I don't *want* to get up in the morning and go to school, but I *have* to."

"I don't *want* to do my homework, but I *have* to."

"I don't *want* to take out the trash, but I *have* to."

"I don't *want* to take that stupid class, but I *have* to."

"I don't *want* to meet curfew, but I *have* to."

"I don't *want* to clean up my room, but I *have* to."

One of the things parents say they don't want to do, but *have* to do, is pay income tax.

Some teachers say that doing paper work is one of the things they have to do, but don't want to do. How do you feel when you *have* to do things you don't *want* to do?

The usual responses to this question are typical upset feelings.

What is the hidden message you send to yourself when you think you are doing something you don't *want* to do, but *have* to do?

The message is that you are *not* your own authority and are *not* in charge of your own life when you do something you don't want to do. Someone else is making you do it against your will.

No wonder you feel so bad.

But wait! Just a minute! Hold on! Stop everything! You've been conned, tricked, fooled. You've *never,* ever, in your entire life done something you didn't want to do.

You just "think" you have.

The fact is you can't do something you don't want to do. It's not possible—*and* you never *have* to do anything.

But don't take our word for it. Let's check it out!

Imagine that the right side of this picture is the "feel good" side. When you're right up against that side, it's 100% "feel good," wonderful, terrific.

Now, the left side of the picture is the "feel bad" side. Over there is frustration, misery, depression. It's "the pits."

Suppose you find yourself somewhere in the middle. Which way would you like to go?

Toward more "feel good," right? Of course, because your basic need is to feel good, physically, mentally, and emotionally.

That is why you always make the choice that you think will give you the *most* "feel good," or

the *least* "feel bad" physically, mentally, and emotionally, *under the circumstances.*

And *you* are the one who chooses what you will do, always.

Sometimes you *enjoy* what you choose to do, such as going to a concert. You could choose to do something else instead. But you always choose to do what you think will give you the most "feel good," under the circumstances.

At other times you don't enjoy any of the choices that seem to be available. For example, when you take out the trash, you may not enjoy doing it, but what do you think the consequences will be if you don't?

You *choose* to take out the trash when the price for not taking it out is too high. You *could* choose to pay the price, however. It's up to you. You're in charge of your life. You're not in charge of what other people do. *They* are.

You don't have to enjoy something to want to do it. We sometimes confuse the words *want* and *enjoy*. We think they mean the same thing. They don't.

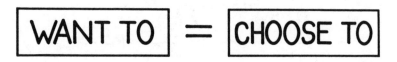

WANT TO = CHOOSE TO

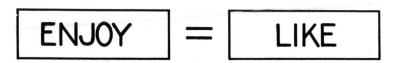

ENJOY = LIKE

Want to means to *choose to. Enjoy* means to *like.*

ARE YOU GOING TO ENJOY THIS?

ENJOY? *NO!!*

If the dentist were to ask you, when you're sitting in the chair waiting to have your tooth drilled, "Are you going to *enjoy* this?" What would you reply? You'd probably say, "No, of course not!"

WANT? YES!!

If the dentist then asked, "Do you *want* me to drill and fill your tooth?" What would you say? If you were there because you had a cavity that was causing you pain, you'd probably say, "Yes, of course! Why do you think I'm sitting here?"

You always do what you want to do *under the circumstances.* You consider the benefits and prices of the different options, and then you *choose* one of the options.

When you get up in the morning and go to school, it is because you have considered the benefits and the prices of the different options, and you *choose* to go to school.

When you do your homework, it is because you would rather do your homework than pay the price for not doing it.

When you take a class you think is stupid, it is because you *want* to *under the circumstances.* You're not willing to pay the price for *not* taking the class.

You consider the benefits and prices involved in meeting curfew or staying out later. When you choose to meet curfew, it's because you are not willing to pay the price for staying out later.

You will clean your room only when you *want* to clean it. Parents may *motivate* you by offering benefits for doing it or prices for *not* doing it, but you are the one who chooses what you do.

The parent who pays income tax does it because it sure beats going to jail.

And the teacher does the paper work because it is better than being out of a job.

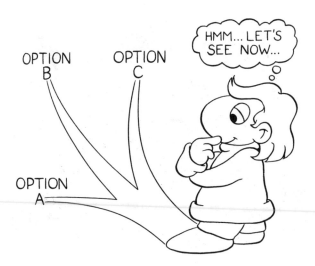

The reality is that parents, teachers, you and I, each of us is responsible for our own life, because each of us chooses what we want to do—and we get the consequences for our choices.

You *benefit* from your wise choices and

you *suffer* as a result of your unwise choices. Even then you are learning and growing in awareness.

The reality is that you are your own authority and in complete charge of your life.

We want you to know that you *always* have a choice, that you never have to do anything *if* you are willing to pay the price for *not* doing it. You can experience a tremendous sense of freedom when you know you have the power to choose.

Since you are the one choosing to do these things, it makes sense to stop telling yourself that you *have* to do them. When you use the words, "have to," the hidden message is that you have no choice. The only time "have to" makes sense is when you add the words "if I want to _____." For example, "I have to study if I want to learn the subject and pass the test."

It's important to know that other people have power also. In fact, parents, teachers, principals, and many others have more power than you do. They have the power to establish prices and benefits, to say what happens when you do or don't do certain things. Those consequences are part of the circumstances you get to choose from. Although you may not like the consequences, you still get to choose from all the choices available under those conditions.

We also want to remind you that you are the one who receives the consequences for every choice you make. There will always be prices and benefits for what we decide to do or not to do. If we choose what will give us the most "feel good" in the long run, our lives will usually run more smoothly, and we'll be happier. If we choose only what will make us feel good right now, we may find ourselves with a heavy price to pay later.

It sure makes sense to us to check out all of our options and choose what's going to be in our best interest in the long run. Don't get us wrong. We're not telling you how to choose. We're just sharing what makes sense to us and hope you'll take some time to think about what you've just read.

CHECK IT OUT

Suggestion: For this and all the other exercises in this book, use separate pieces of paper large enough to give you plenty of room to answer fully and freely.

What is it that I think I don't want to do, but *have* to do?

What would it *cost* me if I didn't do it?

How would I feel if I didn't do it?

Am I *willing* to pay what it would cost?

If the cost of *not* doing it is *higher* than I am willing to pay, it means I really want (choose) to do it.

Experiment a little. When you catch yourself saying "I *have* to _____ _____," replace it with "I *choose* to _____ because I want _____ and I don't want _____.

You always choose what you think will give you the most "feel good" or the least "feel bad" under the circumstances. Remember, although you may not enjoy the circumstances, you don't have to enjoy something to choose it.

CHAPTER TWO

ENJOYING WHAT YOU DO: HOW THE MIND WORKS

What does it take to make you happy?

Some young people say, "I would be happy if my parents would get off my back;"

"stop treating me as if I can't take care of myself;"

"listen to what I'm saying instead of trying to straighten me out;"

"be nicer to my friends;"

"stop embarrassing me in front of my friends."

Some young people say, "I would be happy if my teacher would give me less homework;"

"stop picking on me in class;"

"stop being so boring."

"I would be happy if my friends would stop saying things about me behind my back, things that aren't true."

"I would be happy if I had more friends;"

"if I had my own car;"

"if I got better grades in some classes;"

"if I could express my feelings better;"

45

"if I could keep the commitments I make to myself;"

and on, and on, and on. Why don't you take a few minutes and think of some things that would make you happy.

Remember, during Chapter One, "Accepting Your Own Authority," we discovered that your basic need, my basic need, *everyone's* basic need is to feel good, physically, mentally, and emotionally.

Now, what will it take for you to satisfy your basic need, the one need that all your other needs come from? What will it take for you to feel good?

Why, the answer to that is simple! All you have to do is get your parents, friends, teachers, relatives, neighbors, and the establishment straightened out, so that everyone is doing what you think they must do so *you* can be happy.

NOW HEAR THIS!

How are you doing so far? Do you have the universe under control yet? Trying to bring the universe under control is a tough job.

It takes a lot out of you. At the end of the day you can be very tired, discouraged, depressed, frustrated, sad, or angry.

It seems as though life is not fair—being given a basic need to feel good, *and* having our "feel good" depend on what other people do!

DOES ANYONE HAVE THE POWER TO MAKE YOU ANGRY OR UPSET?

Remember when you answered question number two in the first chapter, "Does anyone have the power to make you angry or upset?"

"Yes!" is the answer practically everyone gives to this question. So, if you answered, "Yes," you are with the majority. There's just one problem, however. Guess what?

You've been conned, tricked, fooled again! *Nobody* can *make* you angry or upset. You are the only one who has the power to do that. Here's how it works.

Our brain's job is to make sure we feel good, mentally, physically, and emotionally.

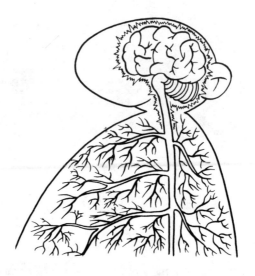

The brain makes the body work by electrical signals that it sends *to*, and receives *from*, all parts of the body.

When the brain senses that our "feel good" is in danger, it instantly gets the body ready for action. That's called stress.

Our glands suddenly release chemicals into our bloodstream. These chemicals strengthen our muscles and quicken our reactions. We get a funny feeling in the pit of our stomach; our heart pounds; muscles are tense. The brain is thinking at high speed, "How can I survive?" Then, suddenly, we take action.

And we survive the danger. Now, an interesting fact is that our body reacts the same way when we get angry or upset about what another person does.

Suppose, for example, that your friend said she would come over to your house to study or to visit at 7:00 o'clock.

When she hasn't shown up by 7:15, you start wondering what happened. You're feeling a little bothered.

By 7:30 you are getting *upset*. You wonder if she forgot. "Why didn't she call to say she'd be late? Some people are so inconsiderate!"

By 7:45 you're really upset. You've been waiting for her for 45 minutes. Does she think that's all you have to do, sit around and wait for her? Now you're really angry.

Probably most people would agree that getting angry or upset in this situation is normal and is to be expected. We have been taught that people can *make* us angry by doing inconsiderate things.

The truth is other people can't make us angry. We make ourselves angry or upset by having a need to control a situation that is out of our control.

When you *think* you can't feel good unless your friend shows up, your brain prepares your body for action. Your glands release chemicals into your blood; your muscles become tense; you are ready to take action to make your friend show up.

Your brain causes your body to react almost the same as if your life were in danger. You're ready to take action.

The problem is, there is no action you can take to make your friend be where she isn't. When your body is under this tension to act without any action you can take, you get frustrated and then angry.

It is *not* the fact that your friend isn't with you that makes you feel bad. It's your *need* for her to be where she isn't that causes you to feel bad.

When you *tell yourself* that you can't feel good when your friend is late, your brain creates stress in your body to do the impossible, make your friend be where she isn't. You'll feel bad until you change your thinking.

When you realize, and tell yourself that you *can* feel good when your friend is late, your brain releases your body from the stress of needing to do the impossible. You may wish your friend were there, but since she isn't you choose to feel good anyway.

You are *not* in charge of what your friend does. You *are* in *complete* charge of how you react to what she does.

Thinking that your "feel good" depends on other people may have started when you were very young.

Because then you really did need other people to feed you, change your diapers, and give you attention. You couldn't do those things yourself.

However, as you got older, you became able to feed yourself,

change your own diapers,

and find your own friends to do fun things with.

Unfortunately, for most of us, our thinking hasn't kept up with the way life really works.

Now, it is possible to change our thinking so we *can* feel good, even when others don't do what we would like them to do.

We might, for example, begin to change our thinking from, "I can't feel good in this stupid class," to "I'm choosing to be here, so I might as well feel good while I'm here. I'll find something interesting about this class."

Or, "I'm choosing to clean my room. I can choose to clean it and feel *bad,* or I can choose to clean it and feel *good.* I think I'll *feel good* while I'm cleaning it."

Parents might change their thinking from, "I can't feel good when I'm doing my taxes," to "I'm choosing to pay taxes, so I might as well feel good while I'm doing this."

Teachers might change their thinking from, "I can't feel good when I'm doing this paper work," to "I'm choosing to be in this job and paper work is part of the job. I might as well feel good while I'm doing it."

In other words, you are not only free to choose *what* you will do, you are also free to choose to feel *bad* or to feel *good* about doing it. It is up to you!

How can we learn to change our thinking so we can feel good more of the time, even when things are happening that we don't like?

It takes a little practice, but you can start right away. Just ask your-self, "How am I feeling right now?"

If the answer is, "I'm feeling good," then that's great!

If the answer is, "Emotionally, I'm feeling bad,"

then ask yourself, "What is happening in my life that I don't like and need to change?"

The next step is to make a list of some things you might be able to do to change the situation. Your list may be long or it may be very short, or there may be *nothing* you can think of to do.

If there is something you can do, check to see if you are willing to do it. Then schedule a time to do it. If there is nothing you can do, or nothing you are willing to do, keep reading. The rest of this chapter will give you a different way to think about emotionally upsetting situations.

Let's take another look at how we make ourselves feel bad by our thinking.

Suppose you are visiting at a friend's house and you've parked your bike outside.

While you are inside enjoying a visit with your friend, a big delivery truck backs into the driveway and accidentally runs over your bike, wrecking it totally.

You don't even know your bike is wrecked. You're still enjoying yourself and feeling good.

So, the fact that your bike is wrecked can't make you feel bad, because it's already wrecked and you're still feeling good.

When you think, "I can't feel good when my bike is wrecked," guess what happens when you see your smashed bike in the driveway?

You feel bad, because you have a need for your bike not to be wrecked. Will feeling bad after you find out your bike is wrecked, return your bike to its original condition? No, of course not!

So, you might as well tell yourself, "I *can* feel good when my bike is wrecked. I wish it weren't wrecked, but it is, and I can't change that right now."

The fact is you have a choice. You can feel bad and have a wrecked bike,

or you can feel good and have a wrecked bike. But one thing's for sure—you have a wrecked bike!

Emotional "feel good" is an overall, satisfying sense of inner peace and well-being. You can't experience this "feel good" when you are angry or upset.

We're not telling you *not* to get angry or upset. When you're upset, you're upset. However, feeling bad doesn't change the situation you're upset about. Remember, it isn't the situation itself that causes you to feel bad or to feel good. It is what you think and say to yourself about the situation that causes you to feel bad or to feel good.

As the wrecked bike story shows, upset feelings are caused by *resisting* what happens. In this case resisting means having a need for your bike not to be wrecked. The most logical way to feel good is to be willing to accept the fact that the situation is *the way it is.* Above all, don't blame yourself for getting upset. Most of us have not been taught to accept "what is," so it may take awhile for you to be able to do it.

Accepting certainly doesn't mean giving up and not doing anything. It just means that you are smart enough to know that since you can't change the situation right now, you might as well feel good anyway. Accepting helps you think more clearly. It also saves your energy for finding the best way to handle the situation itself.

When we say you can choose to feel good in upsetting situations, we are not suggesting, for example, that you throw a party and celebrate the fact that your bike was wrecked. What we are suggesting is that the more you practice using these ideas, the less upset you will become over such things, and the shorter your upsets will be.

The next page gives you some steps to follow to handle being upset about situations in the future.

HOW TO FEEL GOOD

1. Describe the person or situation you are upset about.

2. Brainstorm (by yourself or with someone) and list possible actions you might take to change the situation.

3. Select from this list the actions you are both willing and able to take.

4. Schedule a time for doing each of them.

5. If you want to spend more time brainstorming for other possible actions you might take, decide how much extra time you are willing to spend doing that, and schedule a time for more brainstorming.

Say the following statements to yourself:

6. I now realize, after doing steps 1 through 5, that I've done the best I can at this time to change the situation to my satisfaction.

7. If the situation still isn't the way I'd like it to be, I realize that in order to *feel good* I need to *willingly accept* the situation just the way it is. In other words, just let it be that way for now.

8. I realize I do not have to like or approve of the situation in order to accept the fact that it is the way it is. Acceptance does not mean approval.

9. I realize that if I keep resisting (remain unwilling to accept), I'll feel bad.

10. I realize resisting never changes the situation. I just end up wasting a lot of my valuable time and energy.

11. I realize the power to accept or to resist is mine, and the choice to feel good or feel bad emotionally is also mine — always! I CHOOSE TO FEEL GOOD NOW!

RESISTANCE CHECK LIST

If the following examples are how you are talking to yourself, then you are resisting. Resistance is an unwillingness to accept the fact that something is the way it is. The more you talk to yourself this way, the worse you'll feel.

I don't want to but I have to...
I didn't want to but I had to...
He/she/they made me...
It isn't fair.
Why didn't he/she/they...
Why can't he/she/they...
You'd think he/she/they...
If only he/she/they...
Why am I always the one who...
It shouldn't be this way.
He/she/they shouldn't have...
He/she/they/it make(s) me angry when...
I can't feel good when he/she/they do that.
I should have...
I shouldn't have...
Why didn't I...
If only I had...
I could have done better.
I could have done more.
I could have done it faster.
I can't...
I'll never be able to...
I could never...
It's hopeless.
He/she/they will never change.

CHAPTER THREE

UP YOUR SELF-ESTEEM

Self-esteem determines how much "feel good" you think you deserve to have.

In this diagram, 100% "feel good" is standing up straight to your full height.

When your self-esteem is low, you think you don't deserve very much "feel good." Low self-esteem causes lots of problems for people.

Because, when you *think* you don't deserve to feel good, your mental computer, your brain, causes you to do some things that aren't very good for you. It's a form of self-punishment.

You might say something mean to a friend, and your friend stops doing things with you.

You might not feel like doing your homework, so you get a low grade.

You might stay out late at night, so you get "grounded."

You then have a good excuse to feel bad.

Also, since everybody's basic need is to feel good, when you are feeling bad, you sometimes try to get some short-term "feel good," even if it really isn't good for you in the long run.

That's why some people eat a lot,

take drugs,

or alcohol.

They are looking for a way to escape from their "feel bad."

The problem is that this quick "feel good" doesn't last very long. In a little while the "feel bad" comes right back,

because the "feel bad" is caused by the message in your mental computer that says, "I don't deserve to feel good."

It is possible to change that message in your mental computer and replace it with the message, "I have a right to feel good all the time."

To change this message, we must get rid of certain false ideas that cause us to think that we don't deserve to feel good.

One of these false ideas is, "I've done things I shouldn't have done."

Remember how you answered question number three in the first chapter, "Have you ever done something you shouldn't have done?" Most people answer "yes" to this question.

Thinking that you've done things you shouldn't have causes you to feel ashamed and guilty because of past mistakes and failures.

And these feelings drain your energy so you don't have very much energy left to do what you know would be good for you.

It may have started when you were very young and one of your parents became angry and upset because you did something they didn't like.

Just before that happened everything was fine.

Your mental computer, your brain, was doing a good job satisfying your basic need to feel good. Everything was fine until

you made a mistake. Then, suddenly your mother was shouting at you in an angry voice. Your body went into stress. You were scared.

Your mental computer tried desperately to find out what went wrong.

Because you had been feeling good until you spilled your milk, you mentally hooked up feeling bad with the mistake of spilling your milk.

Maybe one day, while playing in the house, you accidentally broke a lamp. Again, you had been feeling good until you broke the lamp, so

you mentally hooked up feeling bad with making the mistake of breaking the lamp.

Or you may have slammed the door one day, when your dad had a headache. Once again, your "feel good" suddenly changed to "feel bad," so

you mentally hooked up feeling bad with making the mistake of slamming the door.

At other times, you may have mentally hooked up feeling bad with failing to do something that was expected of you.

And if these kinds of experiences happened a lot, especially when you were very young, you may now have reached a point where you automatically feel bad any time you make a mistake or fail at something.

And since your basic need is to feel good, your mental computer tries to figure out how it can help you to feel good again.

It *remembers* what you were told each time you made a mistake or failed, "You *shouldn't* have done that."

The message your mental computer gets is this, "You don't deserve to feel good unless you go back and *not* do what you did."

So your mental computer wants you to go back into the past and change what you did.

But that's impossible. It can't be done. You can't go back and change the past, but you think you *must* change the past or you can't feel good. Thinking you shouldn't have done something is very frustrating.

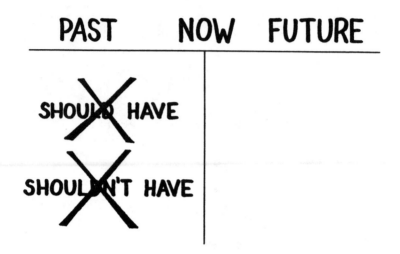

It's also a false idea, because the word "should" does not apply to the past.

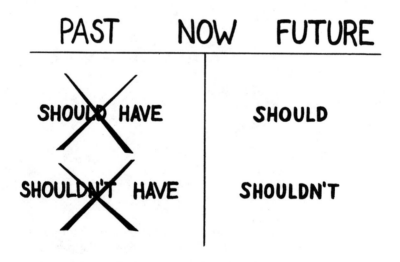

It only applies as advice for the future,

ADVICE FOR FUTURE

YOU SHOULD _____ ,
(ACTION)

IF YOU WANT _____ .
(RESULT)

when used with the word "if."

ADVICE FOR FUTURE

YOU SHOULD

IF YOU WANT

For example, "You *should* study, *if* you want good grades,

ADVICE FOR FUTURE

YOU SHOULD

IF YOU WANT

or, you *should* eat nutritious food, *if* you want good health."

The word "should" only makes sense *before* you've made your decision,

not after you've made your decision and gotten the results. Then you no longer have a choice; you've already made it; it's over with.

You might as well learn from the past and let go of it, because you can't go back and change your decision. Now what's your next choice going to be?

You may have done some things that were not very wise, but you've never done something you shouldn't have done, because "should" does not apply to the past.

It isn't the fact that you made a mistake that causes you to feel bad. It is your thinking that you "shouldn't have" done it that causes you to feel bad.

Another false idea that causes us to think that we don't deserve to feel good is, "I could have done better."

When you get upset with yourself because you made a mistake,

you think to yourself. "I *could have* done better. I don't deserve to feel good because I didn't do what I could have."

The fact is, you did what you *thought,* at the time, would give you the most "feel good,"

or the least "feel bad," physically, mentally, and emotionally.

IF you had been motivated to act better, *THEN* you *could* have acted better.

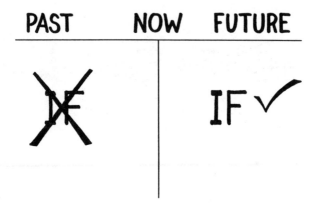

But "ifs" don't apply to the past. You *weren't* motivated to act better. You were motivated to act the way you acted, so there is no way you *could have* acted better.

The fact is you did the very best you could have done with the knowledge and motivation you had at the time.

And you are still responsible for what you did because you get the consequences, whatever they are.

Another false idea that causes us to think we don't deserve to feel good is, "I am what I do."

This idea is very easy to check out. In school we are shown how to diagram a sentence. For example, which word is the subject in the sentence, "Scott rides a bike"?

The subject of the sentence is *Scott.* The subject is the actor in the sentence. Now, which word is the verb in this sentence?

The verb in this sentence is *rides.* The verb is the action word.

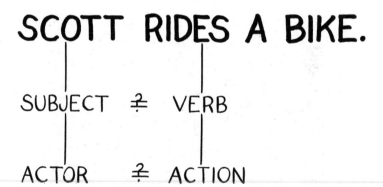

Now, in a sentence, is the subject of the sentence the verb of the sentence?

SCOTT RIDES A BIKE.

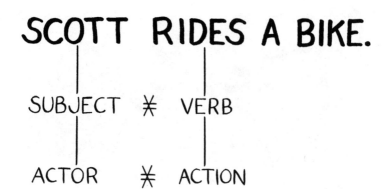

SUBJECT ✳ VERB

ACTOR ✳ ACTION

I AM **NOT** WHAT I DO!

No, of course not! The subject is not the verb. The subject is the subject, and the verb is the verb. Therefore, the actor is not the action, and you are *not* what you do!

Another way to look at it is this—if you *are* what you *do,* then

when you stopped doing it,

you would disappear.

Even though you are not what you do, you are responsible for what you do, because you get the consequences.

When you get rid of the false ideas that you "should have" done better in the past, that you "could have" done better in the past, and that you "are what you do,"

the way you talk to your mental computer will change from "feel bad" self-talk to "feel good" self-talk.

This positive self-talk will help you to feel good more of the time, and to say and do what is in your own best interest.

More and more, as you replace the old "feel bad" self-talk with the new "feel good" self-talk, you will know that you have the choice to feel good all the time. You will realize that you have always done the best you could have done with the knowledge and motivation you had at the time. Your self-esteem will increase and you will have more "feel good" in your life.

The following suggestions will help you choose to feel good more of the time.

1. Substitute "wish" or "rather" for the word "should." For example, instead of saying, "I should have studied for that test," you might say, "I wish I'd studied for that test so I'd have a better grade," or "I wish I hadn't said that mean thing" instead of "I shouldn't have said that mean thing." You also might say, "I'd rather clean my room because I don't want to pay the price for not cleaning it" instead of "I should clean my room."

2. Remember that you are *always* doing the *best* you can at any given moment. Your knowledge and motivation cause you to do what you do, and they are what they are at the moment you act. When you're motivated to do something it means you'd rather do that than something else. That's not to say your actions won't be different in the future. When we say you couldn't have done better, we're talking about the *very instant* you did whatever you did. We are not talking about your ability to act differently or more wisely in the future.

The trap a lot of people set for themselves is judging and blaming themselves for past mistakes with their new knowledge and motivation, knowledge and motivation they didn't have in the past. That makes about as much sense as blaming yourself for not making a cherry pie when all you had available were apples. You had what you had to work with and that's that. There are two smart things you can do with the past: learn from it, and then let go of it. Instead of blaming yourself for your mistakes, you correct them if possible; feel good about yourself, and move ahead with your life.

3. Another helpful idea to keep in mind is that you are *not* what you do. This means you are *not* stupid if you do a stupid thing. What it means is that you acted unwisely, and guess what? It's you who pays the price for what you did. If you continue to think you are stupid, you'll probably keep doing stupid things.

To improve your behavior in the future you'll need to think of yourself as you truly are—a wonderful, precious being. Remind yourself that you are a worthy and important person, worthy and important no matter what you do or don't do, no matter what you have or don't have, no matter what you know or don't know, no matter what you look like.

Keep telling yourself that you have a unique and precious gift to share with the world, and if you weren't here the world would be a little poorer.

Go look at yourself in the mirror. Look deeply into your eyes and say aloud to yourself, "I am a worthy and important person." Say it over and over as many times as you like. Shout it if you want to. When you are finished, give yourself a big smile and a big hug, and go share your gift. And remember, *you* just being *you* is enough of a gift for anyone.

CHECKING YOUR SELF-ESTEEM

The following evaluation deals with a very important subject, your self-esteem. The statements tell something about how you feel and act in different situations in your life. They will help you get to know yourself better.

At the top of the evaluation you will find a list that tells you ways to score each statement. It's a good idea to read each statement carefully and then put down the score that *first* comes to mind. It is important *not* to give the score too much thought, but rather let your inner feelings guide you. When you do that, you will get the score that is truest for you.

It's also important for you to know that this is *not* a test. This is for your information only, and it is important that you *do not* compare your scores to the scores of anyone else. Your scores are simply your opinion of how you feel and act *now.* They could be different tomorrow, next week, or next month. It will be the same for everyone else's scores, too.

You may wish to rescore yourself from time to time; in other words, compare the opinions of the feelings and actions that you had before with the ones you have now.

The higher your score is:
　　the more comfortable you are with yourself;
　　the more regard you have for yourself;
　　the higher your self-esteem.

SELF-ESTEEM EVALUATION

Scoring: Each score shows how true or how much of the time you think that statement is true for you.

> 0 = Never true
> 1 = Somewhat true or true some of the time
> 2 = Fairly true or true about half of the time
> 3 = Mainly true or true most of the time
> 4 = True all of the time

_____ 1. I feel I'm as good as others, even if they are more popular or have better luck.

_____ 2. I feel good about myself, even if others don't pay attention to me.

_____ 3. I accept what happens to me without blaming others.

_____ 4. I feel good about myself, even when people say mean or untrue things about me.

_____ 5. I know I have a right to feel good all the time.

_____ 6. I feel good about myself, even if other people don't like what I do.

_____ 7. I feel good about myself, even when others do something better than I do.

_____ 8. I feel good about myself, even when I lose or make mistakes.

_____ 9. I am able to do things without bragging.

_____10. I speak up for my own ideas and things I like or don't like.

_____11. I feel free to do what I want, even though it may not please other people.

_____12. I feel comfortable with people I meet for the first time.

_____13. I am honest with myself and others.

_____14. I am a good listener.

_____15. I feel good about myself, even when others disagree with me.

===== Total Score

Adapted with written permission of the author, from Barksdale Self-Esteem Evaluation for Students, copyright © 1977 by Lilburn S. Barksdale.

CHAPTER FOUR

CREATING WHAT YOU WANT: GOALS, IMAGING

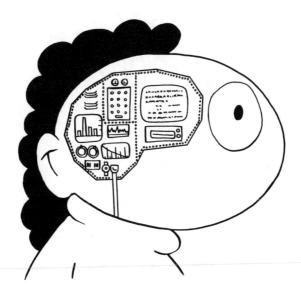

Inside your head is the most powerful computer in the world, the human brain.

Your brain, with its nervous system, operates 24 hours a day, 7 days a week. Its job is to serve you in satisfying your basic need to feel good.

When you were a baby, your brain operated automatically. If your stomach was empty, it caused you to cry until someone fed you.

It still works for you automatically in many ways. For example, it takes care of your breathing, so you don't need to remember when to inhale and when to exhale.

It controls your digestion. Even when you make its job difficult, it will do its best to handle what you give it.

Besides what it does automatically, your brain can also do a lot of other things for you, if you *tell it what you want.*

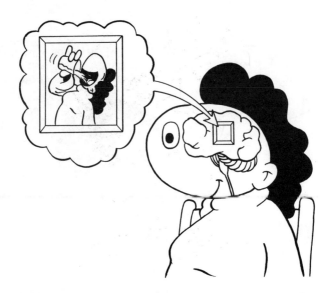

You tell it what you want by creating in your mind a mental picture, or image, of what you want, as if you already had it.

Your brain then causes your body to take action to make your image actually happen. You get up from your chair; go to the refrigerator; get out the milk; pour a glass full, and

your mental picture has now actually happened. You're drinking the milk. This is how your brain runs your body, using mental pictures.

Even when you are sitting in a chair, you can't get out of the chair unless you first have a mental picture, or image, of yourself getting out of the chair.

Your brain is a mental computer that runs your body, and *you* run your brain by choosing images of what you want to do or have in your life.

Suppose, for example, that you've been thinking how nice it would be to have your own guitar. But it costs more money than you want to spend.

Then, one day you decide you are *willing* to pay the price to get a guitar.

When the mental picture of you owning your own guitar is impressed on your brain, your brain starts to make it happen.

It causes you to make a plan.

Then it makes you want to take action on your plan. That's called motivation. You find a job after school, and go to work.

If something comes along that might keep you from reaching your goal, your mental computer will remind you of the image and motivate you to keep acting on your plan.

Sometimes other people seem to tune in to your image and want to help you to make it happen.

Eventually, you will save enough money to pay for the guitar. When you buy it, your image will have really come true.

The reason you have, or don't have, many things in your life now is because of the pictures put into your mental computer from the time you were a baby.

If some things in your life are not how you would like them to be, you can change them by creating new images in your mental computer.

Changing your life is a lot like planting a seed. It takes time, just as a plant takes time to grow from a seed. The change starts to happen, however, as soon as you are *willing* to have it in your life.

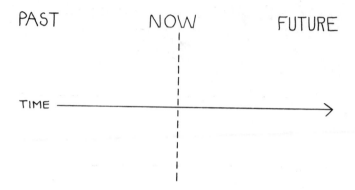

Here is another way to look at how we create situations and things in our lives. Imagine that the line in the middle represents time. On the left is the past; on the right is the future, and in the center is *now*.

PAST   NOW   FUTURE

```
┌─────────────────────────────────────────┐
│        PHYSICAL  REALITY                  │
└─────────────────────────────────────────┘
```

TIME ——————————————————————————→

Above the line represents *physical reality,* things we can see, measure and feel.

PAST   NOW   FUTURE

```
┌─────────────────────────────────────┐
│      PHYSICAL   REALITY             │
└─────────────────────────────────────┘
```

TIME   ─────────────────────────────→

```
┌─────────────────────────────────────┐
│      MENTAL   REALITY               │
└─────────────────────────────────────┘
```

Below the line represents *mental reality,* the images or mental
seeds that we have put into our mental computer, our brain.

PAST   NOW   FUTURE

```
┌─────────────────────────────────────┐
│      PHYSICAL   REALITY             │
└─────────────────────────────────────┘
```

REPORT CARD
C

TIME   ─────────────────────────────→

```
┌─────────────────────────────────────┐
│      MENTAL   REALITY               │
└─────────────────────────────────────┘
```

Many of the situations and things you have in your life *now*

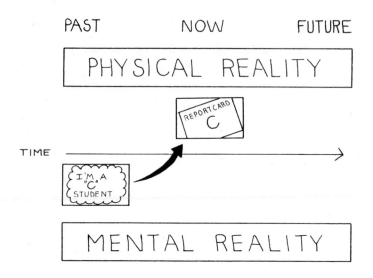

are there because of the mental pictures and thoughts you had in the past.

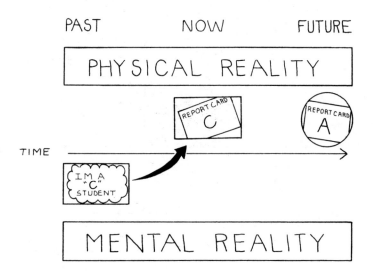

If you want your life to be different in the future,

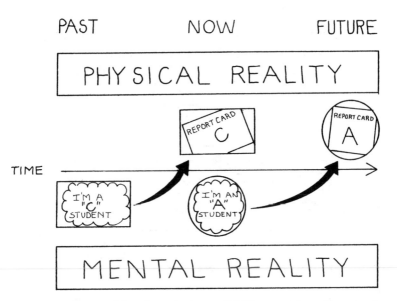

PAST   NOW   FUTURE

PHYSICAL REALITY

TIME

MENTAL REALITY

you can change it by changing your thinking and imaging *now,* by turning your attention to the new situations or things you want to have in the future.

That can be hard to do when you are feeling bad about the way your life is *now,*

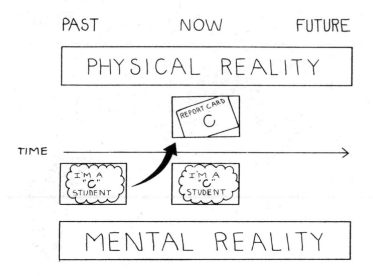

because then you are keeping the mental image of the *way it is now.*
By thinking about it, talking about it and feeling bad about it,

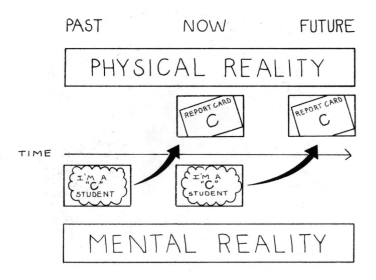

you are actually making sure the situation stays that way in the
future.

To change something in your life that you don't like, you must first be willing to accept the way it is now, and let it be that way for now,

because when you *think* situations that you don't like and can't change have the power to make you feel bad,

you find yourself feeling bad and wasting a lot of valuable energy. You end up mentally fighting situations you can't change, instead of

turning your attention and your energy to creating a mental image of the way you would like your life to be, as if it already *is* that way.

Creating desirable changes in your life takes four steps.

Step number one is, "Know where you are."

Step number two is, "Don't resist."

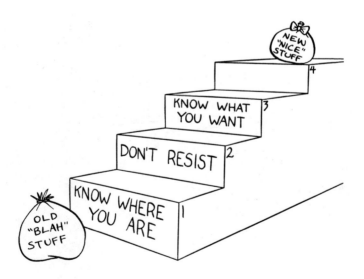

Step number three is, "Know what you want."

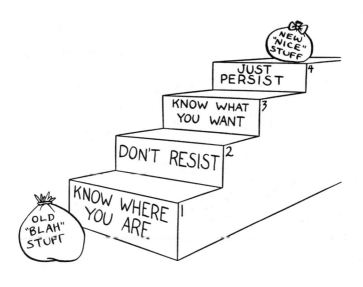

Step number four is, "Just persist."

You might like to think about the different areas of your life and check out how satisfied you are with them.

After you know how you feel about the different areas of your life, the next step is, "Don't resist."

To resist means to fight something mentally even though you are not able to change it.

It really isn't what's happened in your life that makes you feel bad. It is your resistance, your mind refusing to accept what has happened that causes you to feel bad.

When you can *let go* of your *need* to change things you *cannot* change, you will have completed step number two,

"Don't resist." You will feel better, have more energy available, and think more clearly. You will then be ready for step number three,

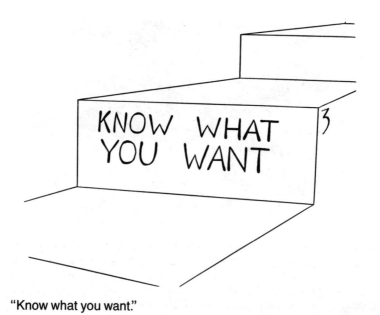

"Know what you want."

This is a very important step, because if you don't choose your own goals in life, your mental computer will come up with some for you, depending on the ideas, values and mental pictures that you've been receiving from others all your life.

It doesn't mean that the ideas, values and mental pictures you've received from others are not desirable. It just means that since you are the one who gets the results for what's programmed into your mental computer, it might be a good idea to check it out and choose what you feel is best for you in the long run.

Your future is not limited by what you have in your life now, *unless* you *think* it is.

You have complete freedom to choose what you want to have in the future.

Sometimes we don't want to think about having new and nicer things in our lives because we are afraid we might be making a mistake.

We might not be able to handle what we get.

Or, we might be giving up something we now have.

The choice is yours. *You* are in charge of your thinking.

And, in the future you will get the results of your present thinking, just as the farmer who plants seeds later on gets to harvest the crop. If you plant corn seeds, you get corn; if you plant tomato seeds, you get tomatoes.

So, what do *you* want to have in the different areas of your life?

Setting goals is easier when you realize that you are free to change your mind any time you want to.

You might try out some goals for awhile, say for one month, and see how they work.

After one month, you might take another look at the goals you set to see if you want to keep them, change them, or get rid of them.

When you know what you want, you are ready for step number four,

"Just persist." In other words, go for it!

Find something you can do right away to get started on reaching your goals.

If you keep picturing your goals as if you've already achieved them, that will cause you to take action,

and keep taking action until you reach your goals.

GETTING WHAT YOU WANT

Here are some suggestions for helping you get what you want. Keep in mind that we don't always know what's in our own best interest at the time. What seems like a good idea may not turn out to be such a good idea after all. Usually, when we want what's best for everybody involved, we are more likely to get what's in our own best interest overall.

1. Know What You Want
   Be specific! Get as clear an idea as possible of what you want to have or do. The clearer you are the greater are your chances of getting what you want. Write down your goal in as much detail as possible.

2. Visualize It
   Imagine what it would look like to be having or doing what you have chosen. How would you look? How would you be feeling? If your goal is a physical object, put in as many details as possible: size, color, shape, texture and so on.

3. Expect It to Happen
   When you truly expect to have or do what you want, this will motivate you to take all the necessary steps to reach your goal.

WHAT I WANT

In each area below, list what you want to have or do.

A. FRIENDS

1._____ 3._____

2._____ 4._____

B. FAMILY

1._____ 3._____

2._____ 4._____

C. SCHOOL

1._____ 3._____

2._____ 4._____

D. PHYSICAL FITNESS

1._____ 3._____

2._____ 4._____

E. CAREER

1._____ 3._____

2._____ 4._____

F. MONEY AND POSSESSIONS

1._____ 3._____

2._____ 4._____

G. OTHER

1._____ 3._____

2._____ 4._____

THINGS TO THINK ABOUT

MY GOAL—the way I'd like it to be:_____

_____

1. What investment (time/energy/money) would I have to make to reach this goal?

2. Am I *able* and *willing* to make this investment?

3. Does this goal *involve* anyone else?

4. Will others involved benefit when I reach this goal?

5. Is it *logical* or *possible* for me to achieve this?

6. Does it *feel right* for me to achieve this?

When you have a clear mental picture of what you want, the next step is to take action. Make a list of the actions you can take, and then start taking them, one at a time. Be open to changing your list of actions as you get new information or ideas. If your goal is a big, long-range one, it will help to divide it into parts, taking one step at a time, keeping the desired goal in mind but focusing your energy and attention on the step right in front of you.

CHAPTER FIVE

PUTTING IT ALL TOGETHER

Remember, we suggested that you approach the ideas in this book by not believing any of them?

Instead, we suggested that you check them out for yourself, using your own experience and your own ability to think. Then, you decide for yourself

whether you want to use these ideas, or tools, to improve the quality of your life, or

choose not to use them.

Remember how we pointed out that everyone has the same basic need to feel good, physically, mentally, and emotionally,

that you always do what you want to do, under the circumstances? You consider the benefits and the costs of all your options,

and then you choose one of the options.

You choose the one you think will give you the most "feel good,"

or the least "feel bad."

You are the one who chooses, always. You are your own authority and in complete charge of your own life.

Many of us have been taught to think that we can be happy only under certain conditions. In other words, we think to ourselves, "I'm not happy now, but I would be happy if things were different."

When we were very young, our "feel good" really did depend on other people. We may think it still does. We then give other people power over our feelings.

The fact is we are in charge of our own feelings.

We are not in charge of what other people do. We *are* in complete charge of how we react to what they do.

It is not so much what happens to us, but how we handle it that causes us to feel bad or feel good.

We covered another area that is very important, self-esteem. Your self-esteem determines how much "feel good" you think you deserve to have.

Thinking you don't deserve to feel good can cause lots of problems in your life.

Sometimes when people feel bad, they try to get some quick "feel good," even if it isn't good for them in the long run.

Thinking you don't deserve to feel good because of past mistakes and failures can drain your energy, and keep you from enjoying your life and from doing what would benefit you.

Fortunately, you can change the message in your mental computer from, "I don't deserve to feel good," to "I have a right to feel good all the time."

You can make this change if you eliminate from your thinking three false ideas.

The first false idea is, "I've done things I shouldn't have done."

The second false idea is, "I could have done better."

And, the third false idea is, "I am what I do." You are not what you do any more than the subject of a sentence is the verb of a sentence.

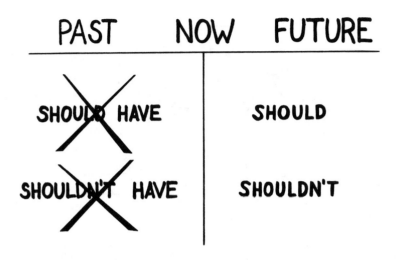

PAST	NOW	FUTURE
~~SHOULD HAVE~~		SHOULD
~~SHOULDN'T HAVE~~		SHOULDN'T

"Should" and "could" don't make sense when talking about the past.

So you may as well learn from your mistakes and move ahead with your life.

And remember, you are responsible for what you do because you get the consequences.

When you realize that you have a right to feel good all the time, that you have always done the best you could with the knowledge and motivation you had at the time, then your self-esteem will increase and you will have more "feel good" in your life.

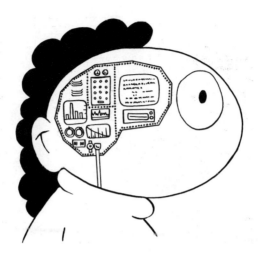

You have the most powerful computer in the world, the human brain, inside your head.

When you tell your mental computer what you want, it will start working to get it for you.

Your brain will help you create a plan and motivate you to act on your plan. It may attract other people to help you.

You have, or don't have, many things in your life now because of the pictures put into your mental computer from the time you were a baby.

Changing your life is a lot like planting a seed. The change starts to happen as soon as you are willing to have it in your life.

You can start to change your life by changing your thinking and imaging now, by turning your attention to the new situations or things you want to have in the future.

To do this, you must stop resisting or mentally fighting the things you have now that you don't like.

Setting goals can be very helpful, even if they are just temporary. It can be fun and very satisfying.

When you "know where you are," and "don't resist," and "know what you want,"

you are ready to "just persist" or "go for it." That's called taking charge of your life!

"FEEL GOOD" SELF-TALK

To assist you further in making your life work for you, in being able to do and have what you want, you might like to use the following "feel good" self-talk. The more you consciously use these phrases, the more often they will automatically come into your mind instead of the old and possibly negative "tapes" you've been hearing from yourself.

These phrases work best when you are totally relaxed, physically and mentally, while repeating them to yourself. You might like to use them every day at a time when you feel this way. Just before getting up and just before going to sleep are usually good times for most people. Some people also like to choose one or two phrases to repeat to themselves whenever they think of them during the day. It's your choice!

I am my own authority and am in complete charge of my own life.

I am always doing the best I can with the awareness I have, and so is everyone else.

I'm in charge of my "feel good."

I accept myself, just the way I am.

I choose to have a happy life.

I appreciate myself.

I am patient, kind, and gentle with myself.

I'm always learning and growing, both from my mistakes and my successes.

I can feel good even when I make a "mistake."

I trust myself.

I'm always OK, no matter what happens or what anyone else says.

I love myself.

We each see things differently; I recognize everyone's right to make their own choices.

I feel good about myself.

I deserve and expect a happy, fulfilling life.

I love and care for myself, and I love and care for others, too.

I learn from my past and move ahead.

I feel warm and loving toward myself, because I know I am a precious being always doing the best I can.

I am not my actions; my actions are simply the means I choose to satisfy my needs.

I care about others, even when I don't like what they do.

I am lovable.

I am my own best friend.

ALSO AVAILABLE ON VIDEO CASSETTE OR FILMSTRIPS!

Taking Charge of My Life: Choices, Changes and Me is based on the innovative program "Taking Active Charge of Your Life" that Ed Harmon and Marge Jarmin developed for groups. It has been helping youth in schools, peer counseling programs, churches, etc. since 1984.

Available in video or filmstrip format, it's a great way to share the ideas and enjoyment of this book with your family, friends, school, church or community outreach program. These life-changing ideas about how we human beings actually operate are organized into five sessions, each with an entertaining video or filmstrip presentation and coordinated exercises for applying the concepts to *real* life.

" 'Taking Active Charge of Your Life' is being received with great enthusiasm by students. Absenteeism is down and the kids look forward to their weekly rap session and a chance to share their feelings. On those days no discipline is required, just excitement."
—Stephanie Insley, M.S., 7th–8th ESL Teacher, San Gabriel, CA

To order or receive information about other self-esteem and stress control materials, telephone or cut out and send the form below to:

> The Barksdale Foundation
> P.O. Box 187
> Idyllwild, CA 92549
> (909) 659-4676

- -

Yes, I want to know more about the kit, "Taking Active Charge of Your Life," and the self-esteem and stress control materials you publish for adults, too. Please send your free information packet to me right away:

Name_____

Address_____

City, State, Zip Code_____

_____ I work with adult groups. Please include information about your materials for independent workshop leaders.